THE HUNDRED DRESSES

by
Eleanor Estes

Teacher Guide

Written by
Anne Troy
and
Jim Stelljes

Note
The Harcourt Brace Jovanovich paperback edition of the book was used to prepare this guide. The page references may differ in other editions.

Please note: Please assess the appropriateness of this book for the age level and maturity of your students prior to reading and discussing it with your class.

ISBN 1-56137-180-7

Printed in the United States of America.

To order, contact your local school supply store, or—

Novel Units, Inc.
P.O. Box 791610
San Antonio, TX 78279

Web site: www.educyberstor.com

Table of Contents

Skills and Strategies

Vocabulary
Antonyms/synonyms

Listening/Speaking
Discussion, drama

Literary Elements
Story elements, characterization, simile, flashback, decisive plot, conflict

Thinking
Brainstorming

Comprehension
Predicting, cause-and-effect, comparison/contrast

Writing
Journaling

Summary

The Hundred Dresses is a touching short novel written in 1944. Although it is over fifty years old, its themes are timeless, and the story relates to contemporary issues. The difficulty of peer acceptance for someone who is "different" and the moral decisions of those who feel peer pressure to conform are enduring themes in children's literature.

The story is about Wanda Petronski, a poor Polish girl from an ethnic neighborhood. She attends a school where she has become the object of scorn and laughter because of an innocent school yard remark.

Maddie is a sensitive girl whose best friend Peggy leads the teasing and unkind joking directed towards Wanda. Maddie spends most of the story reflecting on the history of the joking and, driven by a guilty conscience, finally makes the decision that she will not allow herself to stand by while someone else is the object of criticism, regardless of the peer pressure to do so.

This book lends itself quite naturally to a curriculum concerned with values development and morals education.

Instructions Prior to Reading

You may wish to choose one or more of the following Prereading Questions and Activities. Each is designed to help students draw from their store of background knowledge about the events and themes they will meet in the story they are about to read.

Prereading Questions and Activities

1. Previewing: Have the students examine the title and cover illustration. Also suggest that they flip through the book and look at chapter titles. What do the girls' expressions tell you about their feelings? What do you predict the story will be about?

2. Ask students if they have read any of Eleanor Estes' other books. What was their reaction to these books?

3. Ask students what a "classic" book is. Explain that *The Hundred Dresses* is considered a "classic" short novel.

4. Concept Map: Write "COWARD" at the center of a large piece of paper, to be kept for later comparison with events in the book (or as a bulletin board display to be expanded as the story is read). Have students generate any ideas that come to mind when they hear the term, helping students organize them into categories such as "synonyms," "antonyms," "situations in which students are cowards," etc. Draw "wagon spokes" around the central concept (coward) to connect with the supporting ideas (categories). Encourage students to add to the chart during and after their reading of the novel.

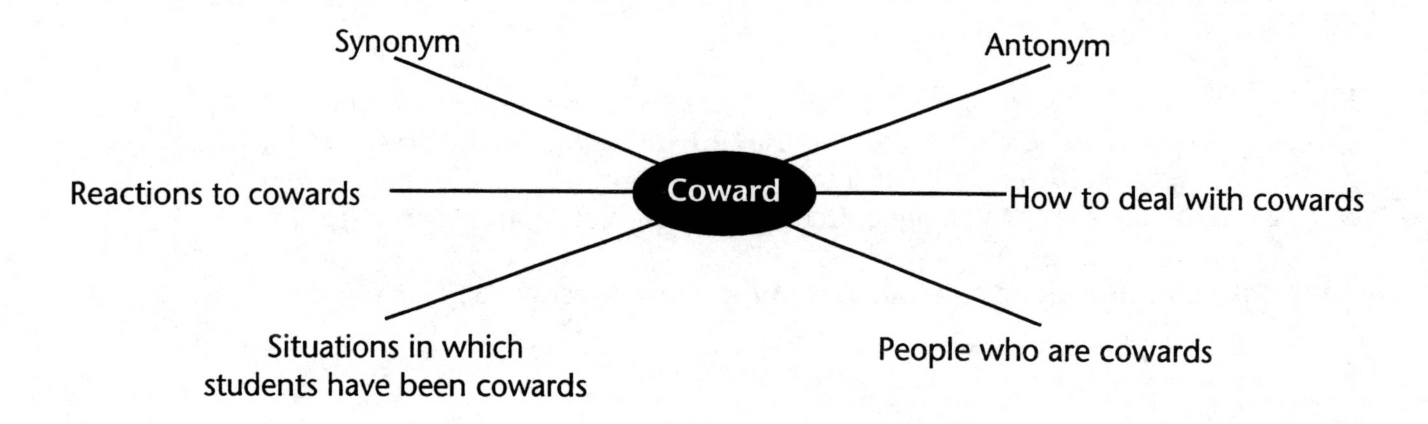

5. The students will keep a response journal. Beyond reading comprehension skills and activities, this study guide suggests meaningful ways in which a student may identify with and relate to the experiences in this book. Pages entitled "Personal Response-Based Questions" should ideally be kept in a private journal and shared only under special circumstances. The rights of students not to share personal reflections should be respected at all times.

Recommended Procedure

Teachers are encouraged to adapt the Novel Unit to meet the needs of individual classes and students. You know your students best; we are offering you some tools for working with them.

Here are some of the "nuts and bolts" for using these "tools"—some of the terms used that will facilitate your use of this guide:

Bloom's Taxonomy: A classification system for various levels of thinking. Questions keyed to these levels may be:

Comprehension questions, which ask one to state the meaning of what is written;

Application questions, which ask one to think about relationships between ideas such as cause/effect;

Evaluation questions, which ask one to judge the accuracy of ideas;

Synthesis questions, which ask one to develop a product by integrating the ideas with ideas of one's own.

Cooperative Learning: Learning activities in which groups of two or more students collaborate. There is compelling research evidence that integration of social activities into the learning process—such as small group discussion, group editing, group art projects—often leads to richer, more long-lasting learning.

This book may be read one chapter at a time using the DRTA, Directed Reading Thinking Activity, Method. The technique involves reading a chapter, and then predicting what will happen next by making good guesses based on what has already occurred in the story. The predictions are recorded, and verified after the subsequent reading has taken place. (See pages 6-7 of this guide.)

Before reading, specific vocabulary words will be pointed out. Students may write simple definitions in their own words before reading. After reading, ask students to redefine the words referring to the context or dictionary. Other vocabulary activities are also included in the unit.

After reading a chapter, brainstorm "what ifs." What if one or another character wasn't in the story, a character did something different, events followed a different sequence or didn't happen at all, etc. The teacher writes all these "what ifs" class responses on the board or a large sheet of paper. At the conclusion of the novel, the review of these "what ifs" may be used in writing a different development and/or ending for the novel.

The Discussion Questions and Activities at the end of each chapter, as well as any Supplementary Activities are provided so that you may, using discretion, make selections from them that will be suitable for use by the children in your group.

Using Predictions in the Novel Unit Approach

We all make predictions as we read—little guesses about what will happen next, how the conflict will be resolved, which details given by the author will be important to the plot, which details will help to fill in our sense of a character. Students should be encouraged to predict, to make sensible guesses. As students work on predictions, these discussion questions can be used to guide them: What are some of the ways to predict? What is the process of a sophisticated reader's thinking and predicting? What clues does an author give us to help us in making our predictions? Why are some predictions more likely than others?

A predicting chart is for students to record their predictions. As each subsequent chapter is discussed, you can review and correct previous predictions. This procedure serves to focus on predictions and to review the stories.

Use the facts and ideas the author gives.

Use your own knowledge.

Use new information that may cause you to change your mind.

Predictions:

____

____

____

____

Prediction Chart

What characters have we met so far?	What is the conflict in the story?	What are your predictions?	Why did you make those predictions?

Graphic Organizers

Graphic organizers are visual representations of how ideas are related to each other. These "pictures" help students collect information, make interpretations, solve problems, devise plans, and become aware of how they think.

Included in the Novel Unit are several types of graphic organizers, such as the Venn diagram, the T-diagram, and brainstorming or cluster circles. A variety of possible answers should be listed by the teacher either on large sheets of paper or the chalkboard. Only then should the students be asked to develop their own graphics. Students are encouraged to express their opinions, and to state what they know about a topic. The teacher lists these opinions and "facts" and later, as the children read and discover that some of their ideas are incorrect, these ideas may be crossed out on the sheets or board. Students should be encouraged to elaborate on their answers, justify their opinions, prove their predictions, and relate what they have read to their own lives.

T-diagrams show likenesses and differences of two characters, plots, settings, etc.

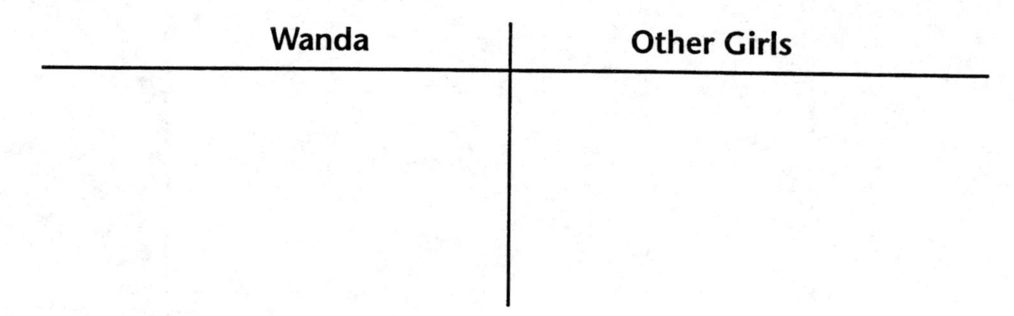

Venn diagrams are taken from math. Characteristics of two characters are listed, and the overlap or similarity may be seen.

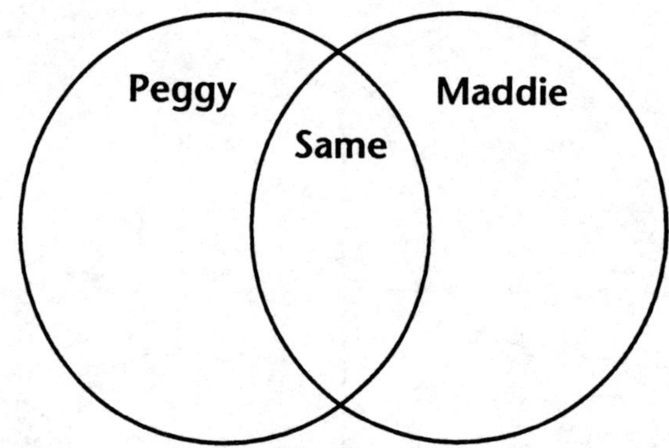

Chapter 1: "Wanda" — Pages 2-7

Vocabulary:

scuffling 3	askew 6	precarious 6	reciting 6
unison 6	session 6	vain 7	perish 7

Vocabulary Activity:

List the vocabulary words on the board or on a sheet of paper in the form of a table. Pronounce the words. Ask the students to rate their knowledge of each of the words as a group or individually:

Word	I Can Define	I Have Heard	I Don't Know

Discussion Questions and Activities:

1. What do we learn about Wanda Petronski? *(was not in her seat, sat in the corner of the room, was not rough and noisy, lived in Boggins Heights)*

2. What does the author mean by "rough boys"? *(page 3)* What might "rough boys" mean today?

3. What do we know about Peggy? *(Page 5, She sat in the front row and got good marks; she was the most popular girl in school; she was pretty; she had pretty clothes and her auburn hair was curly; her best friend was Maddie.)*

4. Why do Peggy and Maddie wait for Wanda every morning before school? *(page 6, to have some fun with her or to tease her)*

5. How would you describe the relationship between Peggy and Maddie? Is this kind of relationship good for either one of them? Why or why not? *(Answers vary.)*

6. Why do you think Miss Mason has her students read the Gettysburg Address aloud every morning? *(Answers vary.)*

Prediction:

What kind of "fun" do you think the kids who are waiting for Wanda liked to have with her?

Supplementary Activities:

1. A story map is an outline that helps you to understand and remember the story better. What do you know about the story after reading only the first chapter?

- What is the setting?
- Who is the main character?
- What is the problem?

As the story is read, more characters may be added and the setting and the problem may change, so additions may be made. Begin to fill in the story map that follows on page 9.

2. Begin attribute webs for Wanda, Peggy, and Maddie. (See pages 12-13 of this guide.)

3. Literary Analysis: A simile is a figure of speech or a comparison of two things using the words "like" or "as." For example: He is as skinny as a toothpick.

   Can you find similes on pages 5 and 6?

   (page 5, "sit there like a frog"; page 6,"as though he were making a touchdown.")

Personal Response-Based Questions:

1. If you were absent from school, who would notice that you were missing?

2. Do you prefer to have a lot of friends in school whom you do not know very well or just a few best friends whom you know very well? Do you know why you feel this way?

3. How would you describe the friends with whom you most often associate? How do they look? How do they act in school? What do they wear? How do they talk?

4. Do you wish your friends were more like you, or do you wish you were more like your friends?

5. Do you think Wanda liked where she sat in the class? Why or why not?

6. Argue for one of the following statements:
   a) Teachers in school should let students sit anywhere they want in class. Best friends should be able to sit together.

   b) Teachers should constantly change seating in class so that everyone gets to know everyone else. No one should feel excluded.

7. Do you have enough friends?

Story Map

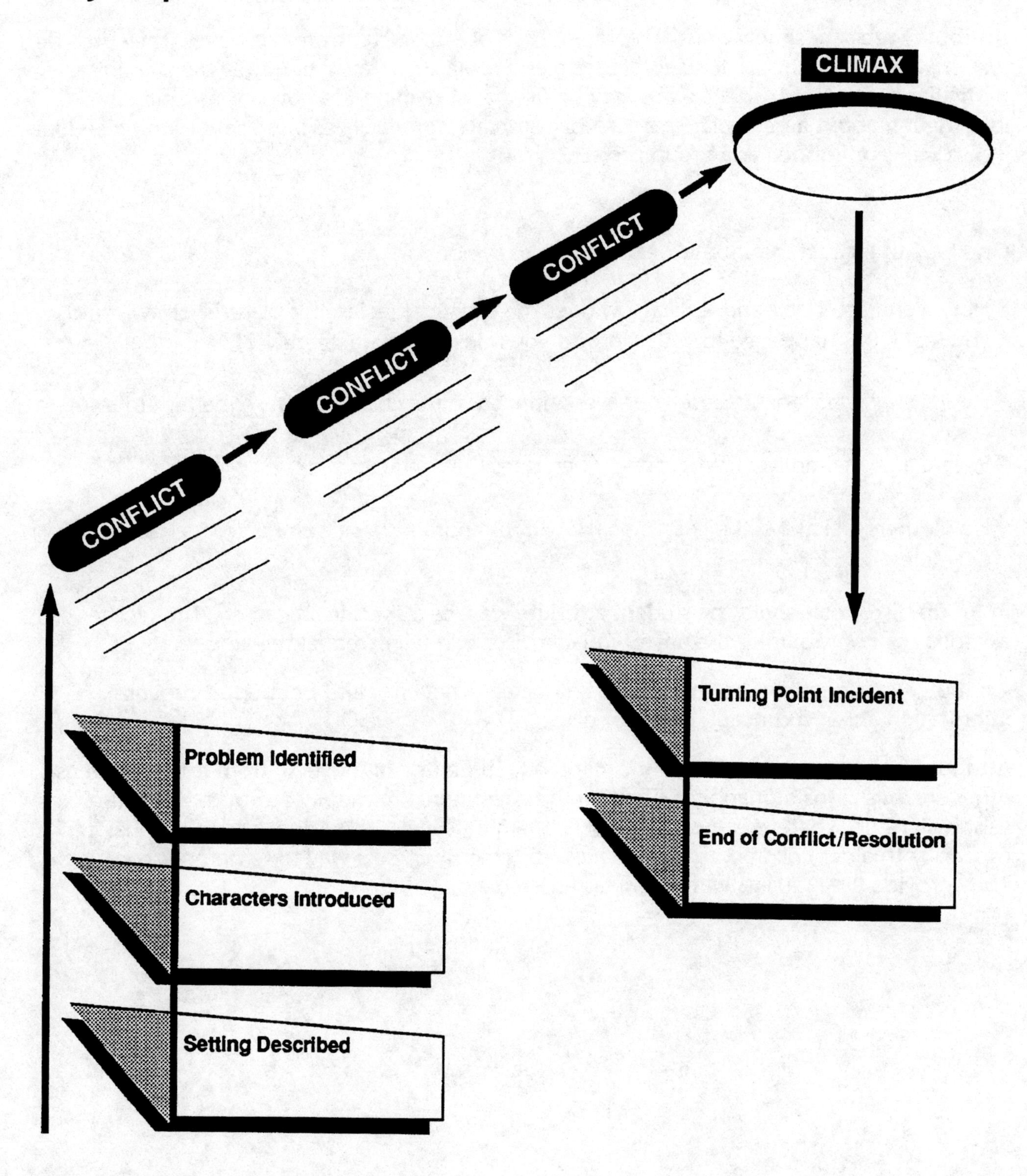

CLIMAX
CONFLICT
CONFLICT
CONFLICT
Problem Identified
Characters Introduced
Setting Described
Turning Point Incident
End of Conflict/Resolution

Using Character Webs—In the Novel Unit Approach

Attribute Webs are simply a visual representation of a character from the novel. They provide a systematic way for the students to organize and recap the information they have about a particular character. Attribute webs may be used after reading the novel to recapitulate information about a particular character or completed gradually as information unfolds, done individually, or finished as a group project.

One type of character attribute web uses these divisions:

- How a character acts and feels. (How does the character feel in this picture? How would you feel if this happened to you? How do you think the character feels?)

- How a character looks. (Close your eyes and picture the character. Describe him to me.)

- Where a character lives. (Where and when does the character live?)

- How others feel about the character. (How does another specific character feel about our character?)

In group discussion about the student attribute webs and specific characters, the teacher can ask for backup proof from the novel. You can also include inferential thinking.

Attribute webs need not be confined to characters. They may also be used to organize information about a concept, object or place.

Attribute webs are a kind of semantic mapping. Students can move on from attribute webs to other creative kinds of mapping. They can be encouraged to modify attribute webs, use subdivisions, in whatever ways are useful to them personally. It is important to emphasize, especially to older children, that attribute webs are just a visual way to remember concepts. They provide the students with a tool to remember.

Attribute Web

The attribute web below is designed to help you gather clues the author provides about what a character is like. Fill in the blanks with words and phrases which tell how the character acts and looks, as well as what the character says and what others say about him or her.

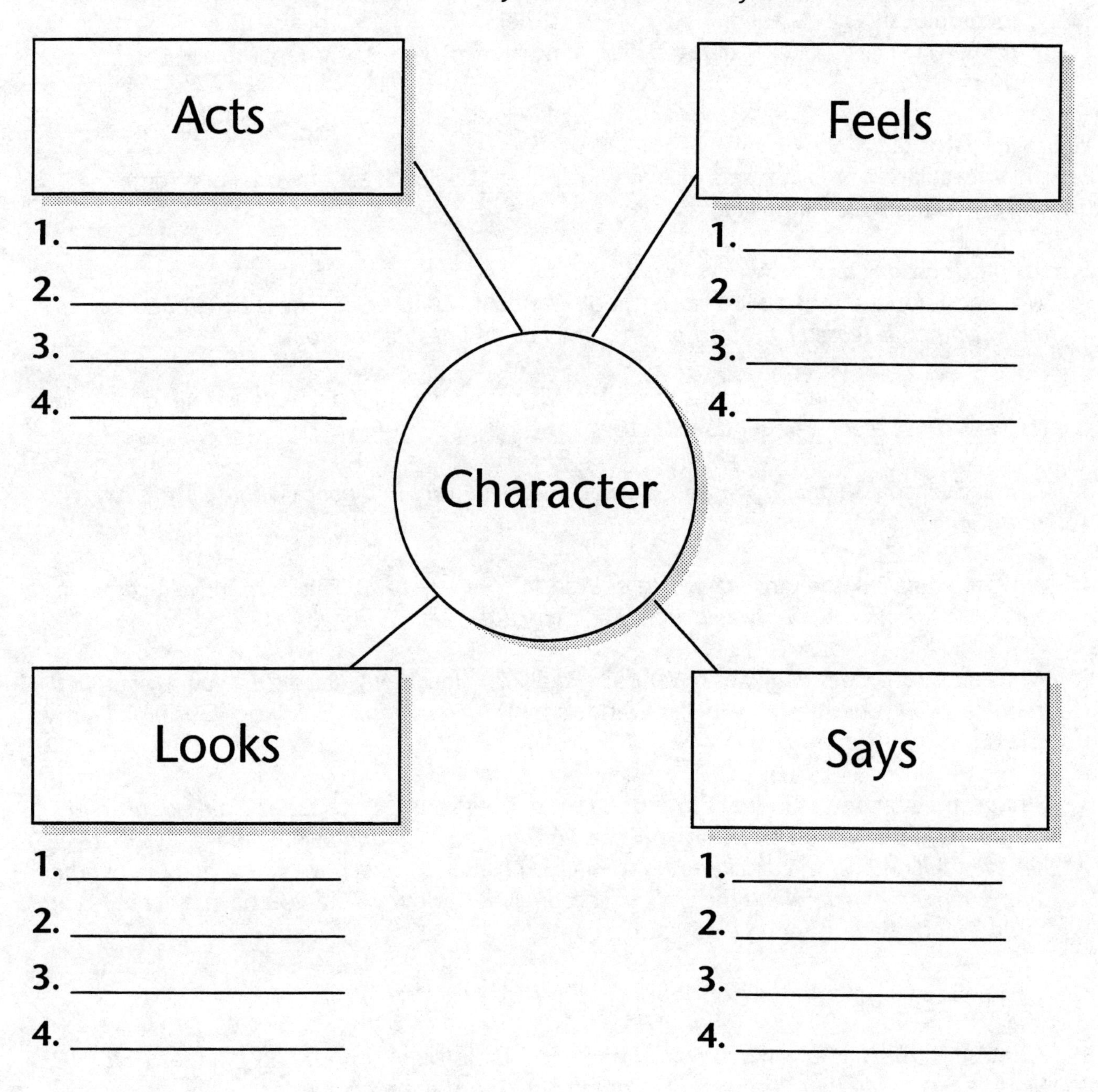

Chapter 2: "The Dresses Game" — Pages 11-20

Vocabulary:

intruders 8	furthermore 8	disgracefully 9	strewn 9
circulated 9	scurry 10	courteous 12	nudge 12
incredulously 12	stolidly 13	shrieks 13	peals 13
derisively 13	exaggerated 15	disperse 16	inseparable 16
mock 17			

Vocabulary Activity:

Put the vocabulary words into sets of two words each. Use each set of words in a sentence. Choose one sentence to illustrate.

Discussion Questions and Activities:

1. What additional things do we learn about Wanda in Chapter 2? *(She is poor, does not have many clothes, is teased by the other girls, and has an unusual last name.)*

2. Would you like to live in Boggins Heights? Why or why not? *(Page 9, It was not a nice place to live because there were rundown houses.)*

3. Who is Svenson? *(Page 9, Svenson is an old man who lives in a house with a dirty, junky yard.)*

4. Why do you think the girls made fun of Wanda? *(Pages 10-12, She didn't have a common name like the other students; her dress was clean but it wasn't ironed.)*

5. What questions does Peggy ask Wanda? *(Page 12, "How many dresses did you say you had hanging up in your closet?")* What is Wanda's reply? *("a hundred")* Why do you think Peggy asked this question every day?

6. What is the reaction of Peggy's friends to these questions? *(Page 13, The girls laughed at Wanda.)* What is Wanda's reaction? *(Page 16, "And finally Wanda would move up the street, her eyes dull and her mouth closed tight, hitching her left shoulder every now and then in the funny way she had, finishing the walk to school alone.")* How would you have reacted? How could Wanda have stopped this teasing game?

7. Maddie seems bothered by this teasing. Why? *(Answers vary.)*

8. What is Maddie afraid will happen if Peggy and the others stop teasing Wanda? *(Page 18, Maddie was afraid that Peggy and the others could start in on her next.)*

Supplementary Activities:

1. Compare and Contrast: Use a compare and contrast chart to illustrate the similarities and differences among Peggy, Maddie, and Wanda. How are they similar? How are they different? Compare, for example, clothes, speech, background, and attitudes of others towards each of them.

	Peggy	**Maddie**	**Wanda**
Where They Live			
Clothes			
Speech			
Background			
Others' Attitudes			

2. Compare and contrast Peggy's and Maddie's attitude towards Wanda using the Venn diagram. How are they similar? How are they different?

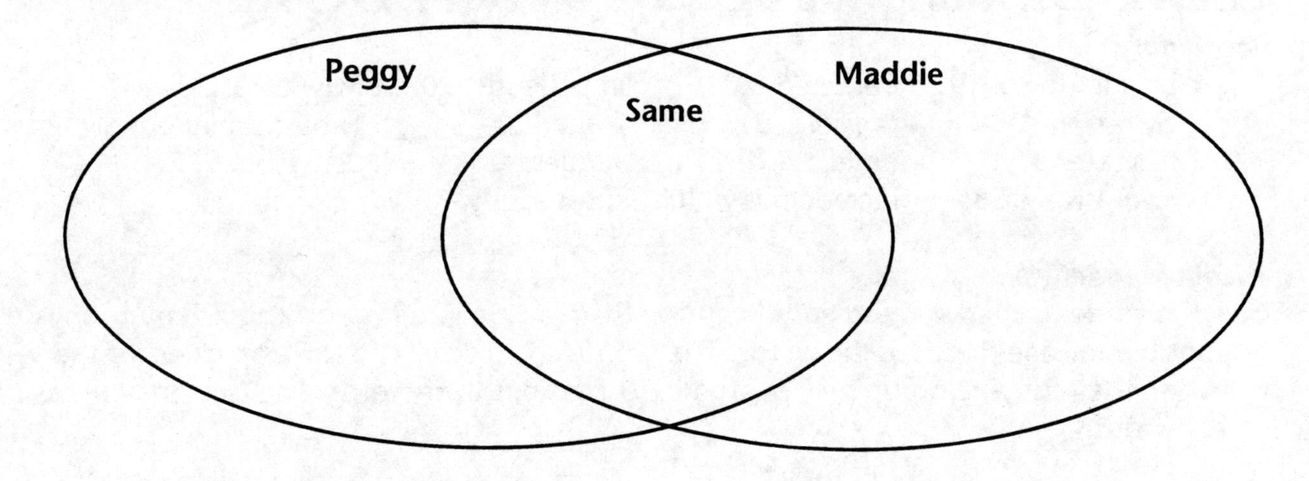

Personal Response-Based Questions:

1. Have you ever been the leader of a group that teased someone? Describe.

2. Have you ever been part of a group that teased someone? Were you proud of being in the group? Were you glad the people were not teasing you? What emotions did you feel at the time? Do you know why you were doing it?

3. Have you ever felt alone or lonely at school? Why? Can you remember the occasion?

4. When was the last time you tried to make a new friend at school?

5. Should school be a place where everyone has fun? Do you think everyone in your class has fun? Why or why not?

6. Is there anything you could do to help everyone have fun? Does everyone join in at recess time and play together?

7. Do you think you would lose the friends you have now if you made some new friends also?

8. Why are people so often afraid to meet new people?

9. On page 16 the author writes, "Peggy was not really cruel." Do you agree or disagree with what the author wrote? Be prepared to defend your answer. What does the evidence suggest?

Chapter 3: "A Bright Blue Day" — Pages 19-33

Vocabulary:

buckle down 19	puckered 20	impatiently 20	vividly 21
crimson 21	precious 22	jaunty 24	absent-mindededly 24
hesitate 24	timid 25	vaguest 25	enveloped 28
impulsively 28	incredulously 30	suspiciously 30	stolidly 31

Vocabulary Activity:

Give the students the word list, and then have them divide into four groups. Each group is responsible for one-fourth of the words. The groups should meet to develop clues for the words on their list. The group may pantomime or act out their words. The class may guess the correct word.

Discussion Questions and Activities:

1. Why is Maddie having a hard time concentrating in school? What is on her mind? *(Page 20, She is thinking about the day Peggy and the group started teasing Wanda.)*

2. When did the hundred dresses game start? *(pages 21-22, the day in October that Cecile wore a new dress)*

3. Why do you think the author uses the word "bright" so many times in this chapter? How many times does she use the word?

4. Why doesn't Jake walk to school every day with Wanda? *(Page 23, He helps the janitor at school with jobs. He probably needs the money from this job to help the family.)* How would this story have been different if Jake had walked to school each day with Wanda and stayed with her until school started?

5. Why do you think Wanda tells the girls she has a hundred dresses? *(page 29)*

6. What is Peggy's reaction when Wanda says, "I got a hundred dresses home"? What is the reaction of the group? *(Pages 30-32, They did not believe Wanda and made fun of her.)*

7. Why does Maddie feel "relieved" when the school bell sounds? *(Page 32, The girls had to run into school and stop the teasing. Maddie did not like the girls being mean to Wanda.)*

8. Literary Analysis: A **flashback** is a device writers use to present incidents that occurred prior to the opening scene of the story. Ask students to locate an example of flashback in this chapter. Point out that flashbacks may be presented in several ways—character's recollection, character's narration, dream sequence—and ask how students would characterize Maddie's flashback. *(recollection)* Ask what purpose this particular flashback serves. *(It provides background information, clarifying how the teasing about the hundred dresses started.)*

Supplementary Activities:

1. Use a Cause-Effect Map or Sequence Chart to map the events in Chapter 3. (See page 18.)

2. Drama: Act out this chapter, especially Wanda's joining the group. Work in groups to write the dialogue based on the book.

3. Make a Decisive Plot Chart. (See page 19 of this guide.)

Cause-Effect Maps:

To plot cause and effect in a story, first list the sequence of events. Then mark causes with a C and effects with an E. Use an arrow from the cause to the effect. Remember that many effects cause something so they might be marked with an E and a C with an arrow to the next effect.

Events in the Story:

1.

2.

3.

4.

5.

6.

7.

8.

9.

10.

Another way to map cause and effect is to look for an effect and then backtrack to the single or multiple causes.

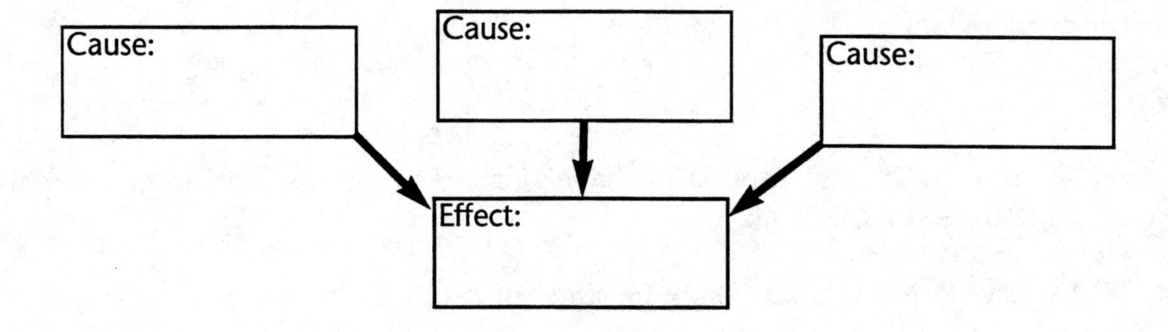

Decisive Plots

In literature, the plot often is carried along by the causes and effects of decisions made by the main character. Had the character made an alternate decision, the plot would have turned in a different direction. Even small decisions can bring about later events.

In the diagrams below, briefly describe a situation in which a decision had to be made, what the decision in the book actually was, and what alternate decision could have been made. Then discuss the results of the decision. Finally, write the changes in the plot that would have resulted, had the alternate decision been made.

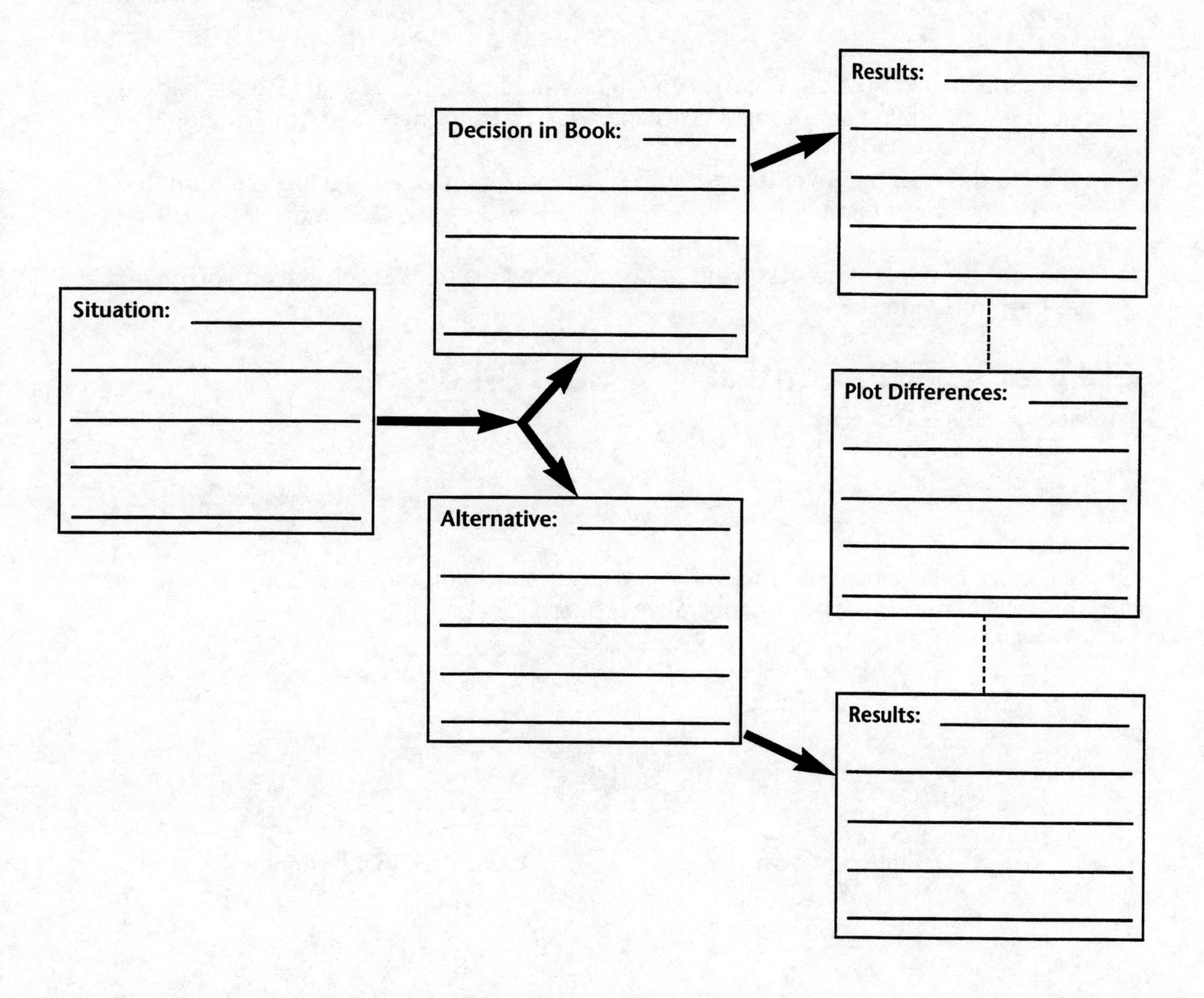

Personal Response-Based Questions:

1. Wanda does not seem to have been bragging or lying about the dresses, but Peggy makes a big deal out of it. Can you remember a time when you said something strange just because you were excited or because you were around people who were excited?

2. Do you think Wanda regretted what she had said? Have you ever wished you could have taken back something you had said? Describe the situation.

3. Can you think of something said to you that you wish someone had not said? Explain. Do you think maybe they really did not mean it, but now, like Wanda, they cannot take it back?

4. Counterfactual Prediction: What do you think would have happened if Wanda had just said she was kidding about the dresses and apologized for her "slip of the tongue"?

5. What do this chapter's events suggest to you about times when you are in a hurry to speak out without thinking?

6. What do you think is the best thing to do when you realize that something you have said has been misunderstood?

Chapter 4: "The Contest" — Pages 34-39

Vocabulary:

shuddered 35 disguise 35 timid 36 cerise 38
consisted 38

Vocabulary Activity:

The students will develop word maps. They will use color to distinguish antonyms, synonyms etc. This activity may be done in cooperative groups.

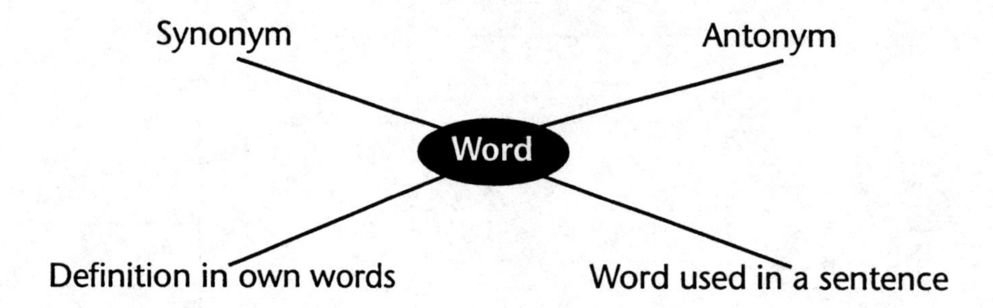

Discussion Questions and Activities:

1. Why is Maddie glad she did not meet Wanda on the way to school? *(Page 34, She did not have to go along with Peggy's teasing of Wanda.)*

2. What keeps Maddie from asking Peggy to leave Wanda alone? *(Page 35, She was afraid she could become a new target for Peggy and the girls.)*

3. Why does Maddie tear up her note to Peggy? *(Page 36, "She was Peggy's best friend, and Peggy was the best-liked girl in the whole room. Peggy could not possibly do anything that was really wrong.")*

4. What other problems did Wanda have in school? *(Page 36, Sometimes Wanda read very slowly before the group and sometimes she just wouldn't read.)*

5. What contest are the girls involved in? *(page 38, drawing and coloring contest)* Who does Maddie think will win the contest? Why does she think this? *(Page 38, Peggy will probably win because she drew better than anyone else.)*

6. Why does Maddie have Wanda's absence on her mind so much? *(Maddie's conscience bothered her that she could not stop Peggy and the girls from teasing Wanda.)*

Personal Response-Based Questions:

1. Have you ever been afraid to speak up when you knew someone was mistreating someone else? Why do you think you were afraid?

2. To "rationalize" means to invent self-satisfying but incorrect reasons for one's behavior. How does Maddie rationalize her behavior towards Wanda? Everyone has probably done this before. Can you think of a time when you rationalized?

3. Many of us are afraid to read or speak before a group. How do you think Wanda feels when she is called upon for oral reading?

4. How do you feel when asked to talk before the class? Can you remember your worst experience of speaking in front of the class? How was it? Would you do it any differently if you had to do it over again?

5. Do you think teachers are ever afraid to speak before the class?

6. During this chapter Maddie has been daydreaming. Do you ever daydream? What is it usually about? Do you think daydreaming is good or bad?

Chapter 5: "The Hundred Dresses" — Pages 40-50

Vocabulary:

lavish 41	exquisite 45	monitor 45	purposely 48
deliberately 48	thoughtlessness 48	stole 49	

Vocabulary Activity:

Have the students locate the words in context and rewrite the sentence from the text to mean the same thing without using the vocabulary word.

Discussion Questions and Activities:

1. What was surprising about the prize winner of the drawing contest? *(Page 44, The winner was Wanda, who had drawn 100 pictures of dresses.)*

2. Why wasn't Wanda able to receive the prize? *(Page 47, She had moved.)*

3. What does Mr. Petronski's letter tell you about him? *(Page 47, He does not write nor probably speak "good" English. He has known how cruel the children have been to his family.)*

4. What reasons does Mr. Petronski give for their moving to the big city? *(Page 47, He hoped in the big city his children will not be made fun of because of their "different" last name and that people will not make fun of them because they are Polish.)*

5. Again Maddie is having a difficult time doing her lessons? Why? What is causing the "sick feeling" Maddie feels in her stomach? *(Pages 48-49, Maddie's conscience is bothering her. She knows she should have stopped Peggy and the other girls in the hundred dresses game.)*

6. Do you think Maddie is responsible for Wanda's moving away? Do you think Maddie is strong enough to stand up to Peggy and the other girls? Would that have made a difference?

7. How is Peggy affected by Wanda's moving away? Do you think Peggy feels even just a little bit guilty? Why or why not?

8. Do you think Miss Mason could or should have done things to help Wanda fit into school?

Supplementary Activities:

1. Complete the Nature of Conflict Chart. (See page 24 of this guide.)

   Possible examples of conflict in the novel:

   - *Wanda vs. the atmosphere at school*
   - *Maddie vs. the atmosphere at school*
   - *Maddie vs. herself*

2. Choose two conflicts from your own life. Describe the conflict, identify the type and describe how it was (or is being, or will be) resolved.

Chapter Six: "Up on Boggins Heights" — Pages 51-63

Vocabulary:

forbidding 51	dismal 51	foreigner 52	assailed 52
pounce 52	consoled 52	drab 53	rickety 54
customary 54	sparse 54	crouching 56	cautiously 57
frail 57	downcast 58	dilapidated 59	loping 59
unintelligible 60	disconsolate 61		

Vocabulary Activity:

Find the base or root word for each vocabulary word. What prefixes or suffixes were added? What is the meaning of the root word? How did the prefix or suffix change it?

Discussion Questions and Activities:

1. What do Peggy's statements about Wanda tell you about Peggy? *(Pages 51-52, Peggy was trying to justify her treatment of Wanda and her game of the hundred dresses.)*

2. What does Maddie want to tell Wanda when she finds her? *(Page 52, They were sorry they picked on her, the whole school thought she was wonderful, and to not move away.)*

3. What does Boggins Heights look like when Peggy and Maddie go there? *(page 51, "the part of town that wore a forbidding air")*

4. What do Maddie and Peggy find out when they reach Wanda's house? *(Pages 56-57, She has moved and the house is empty.)*

The Nature of Conflict

As is true in real life, the characters in novels face many conflicts. When two people or forces struggle over the same thing, conflicts occur. The excitement in novels develops from the use of the three main types of conflict: (1) person against person, (2) person against nature or society, and (3) person against himself.

Below list some of the conflicts from the novel. In the space provided, briefly describe the conflict and indicate which type of conflict is involved, printing "PP" for person vs. person, "PN" for person vs. nature or society, and "PS" for person vs. self. Then choose three of the conflicts and describe how each was resolved.

Conflict	Description	Type

Conflict #1 resolution: ______________________________

Conflict #2 resolution: ______________________________

Conflict #3 resolution: ______________________________

5. How does Peggy feel about Wanda now? *(Page 62, "She's gone now, so what can we do? Besides, when I was asking her about all of her dresses she probably was getting good ideas for her drawings. She might not even have won the contest otherwise.")* What does this say about Peggy?

6. After doing "the hardest thinking she had ever done," what decision does Maddie make? *(Page 63, "She was never going to stand by and say nothing again. If she ever heard anybody picking on someone because they were funny looking or because they had strange names, she'd speak up. Even if it meant losing Peggy's friendship...")*

Supplementary Activities:
Complete a Cause and Effect Concept Map as shown on page 26.

Personal Response-Based Questions:
1. We all have had a guilty conscience at one time or another. Maddie has been unable to find Wanda and apologize to her. Have you ever been unable to say you were sorry to someone? How did you feel at the time? Did you, like Maddie, promise yourself it would not happen again?

2. Do you think the longer you wait to apologize the harder or easier it makes it to do? What does this suggest to you for the future?

3. Maddie is no longer afraid of losing her best friend if she should speak up against hurting someone. Do you think she would lose her friend? Would she be a friend worth having if she acted that way?

4. Think about someone you know. What was he like when you first met him? What have you found out since meeting him that changed your opinion of him? Was it something he said, did, or felt? Or was it something that someone else told you about him?

Chapter 7: "The Letter to Room 13" — Pages 64-80

Vocabulary:

intently 70	equalize 72	cornucopias 73	brilliancy 76
hastily 77	vivid 78	clattered 79	stolidly 80

Vocabulary Activity:
Ask the students to "guess" at the meaning from context of each vocabulary word, telling why for each guess. Make a list of the "why answers" to teach context clues.

Concept Map: Cause and Effect

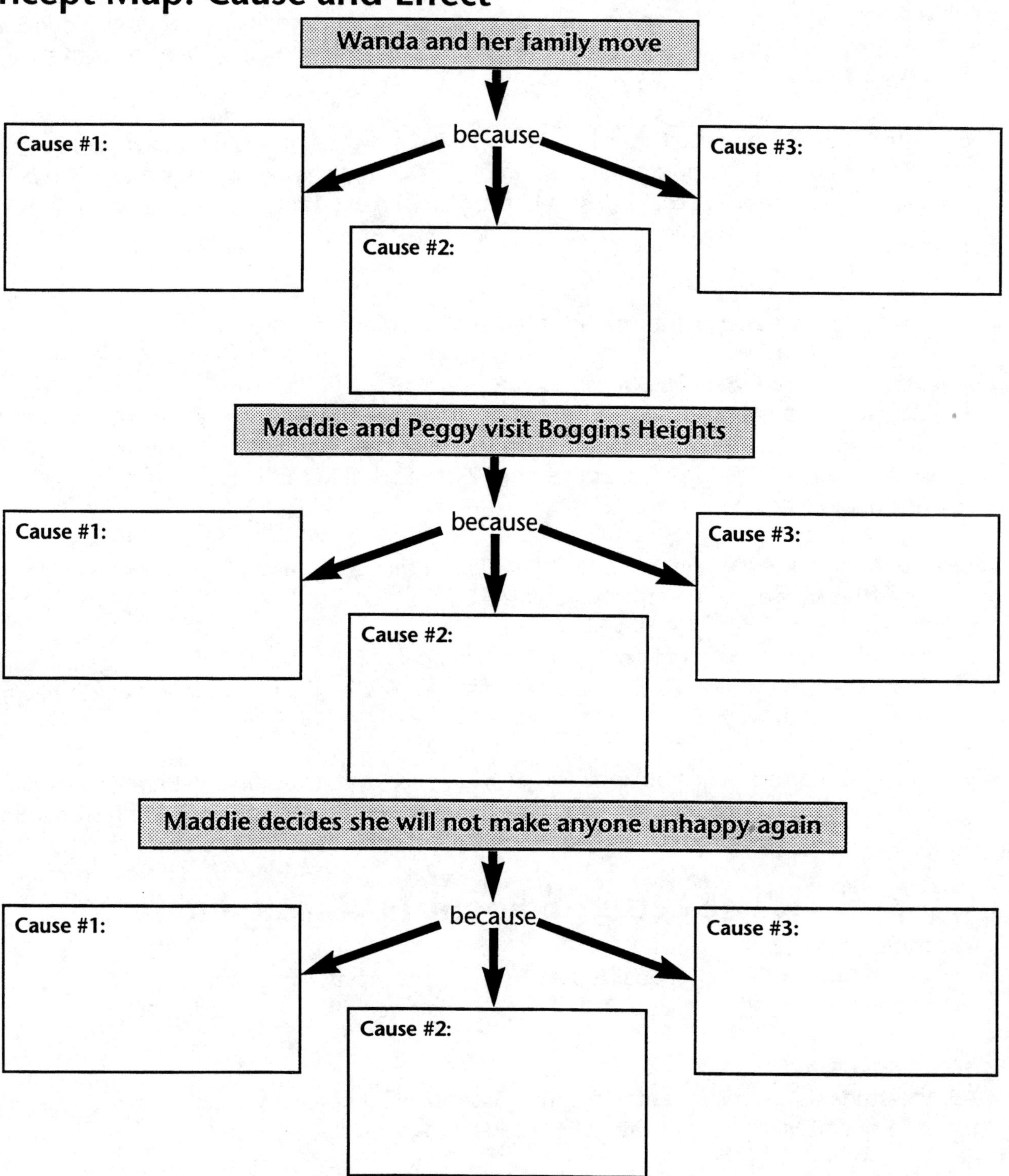

Discussion Questions and Activities:

1. What do Maddie and Peggy send to Wanda? *(page 64, a friendly letter)* Why do you think they didn't say they were sorry for the way they treated her?

2. Why do you think Wanda wrote a letter to Room 13?

3. How does Wanda feel about where she is living now? *(Page 72, She said the school and the teacher are not as good as Room 13.)* What do you think Wanda means by, "my new teacher does not equalize with you"? Do you think she means it?

4. What discovery does Maddie make while studying the pictures Wanda had drawn? *(Pages 78-80, The pictures really looked like Maddie and Peggy.)*

5. How do you think Maddie really feels at the end of the story? *(page 80)*

Supplementary Activities:

1. Writing a Friendly Letter: A friendly letter is a nice way to write to someone who is faraway. In a friendly letter it is fun to share your experiences, thoughts, and feelings with someone you know.

   Practice your letter writing by writing a letter to Wanda. Pretend you are a student who is in Room 13. You might tell Wanda of any new happenings in the class. Have you noticed any change in Peggy or Maddie?

2. Maddie and Peggy were good friends. They shared many experiences together—good and bad. Think about the best friend you have had. Describe that friendship, including both high and low points.

Personal Response-Based Questions:

1. The last chapter of this book takes place at Christmas. Why do you think the author did it this way?

2. Do you feel that Wanda has forgiven the girls for the way they treated her? What makes you feel this way?

3. Peggy does not seem aware that she has hurt Wanda's feelings. Do you agree?

4. Do you think it is possible that we hurt other people without ever knowing it?

5. Have your feelings ever been hurt by someone who maybe did not realize they were doing this to you?

6. What would you tell Wanda if you could? What would you tell Maddie if you could?

7. Which of these people is most like you?

8. Which of these people would you most like for a friend?

Postreading Questions and Activities

1. Summarize the story using the story diagram below. What purpose is there in a story diagram? How would using a story diagram help an author?

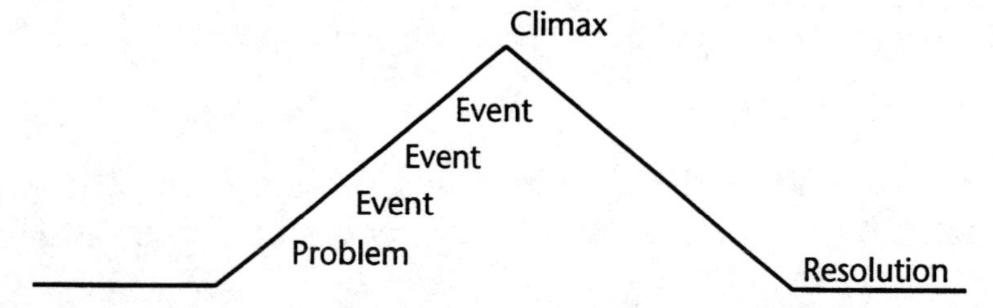

2. Characterization: Characters are developed by what they say, think, and do and by how others in the novel react to them. Review the attribute webs. Which characters in this novel provided wisdom and perspective? How did the characters change during the story? How would you explain the changes?

3. Is there a heroine in this story? Can a heroine have some bad character traits?

4. The setting (time and place) is important in this story. Could the author have presented this same theme in another time and place? What other setting could have been used?

5. Theme is the novel's central idea. What is the author's message? Why do you think the author wrote this story? What do you think is the most important thing to remember about this story? Support your ideas for the theme or themes by examples from the novel. Is the central theme of this story presented directly or indirectly?

6. Were you disappointed in the ending of the novel? How do you think it could have been improved?